One Cl House

Susan Ring
Illustrated by Julie Olson

Rigby®

A Harcourt Achieve Imprint

www.Rigby.com
1-800-531-5015

Mom and Dad were going away
for one week.

Grandpa would stay with the twins,
Sara and Sam.

Mom said, "Grandpa, while we are gone,
please don't make any inventions."

"Don't worry," laughed Grandpa.

"Woof," barked Simon.

Grandpa often made silly inventions.
Once he made some special shoes
for Simon.
The shoes cleaned the floor,
but they were slippery.
Simon slid right out the front door!
He never wore the shoes again.

The twins loved having Grandpa stay
with them.
Each day they did something fun.
They even rode bumper cars at
the fair!

The twins and Grandpa were having
a great time.
They didn't worry about dirty clothes
or dirty dishes.
They didn't worry about crumbs
on the floor.

One day Sara looked at the calendar.
She said, "Hey! Mom and Dad
come home tomorrow!"

"Oh, no," cried Sam, "look at this mess!"

Grandpa said, "We need to get busy cleaning."

Sara said, "I'll mop the floor."

Sam said, "I'll wash the clothes."

"Woof!" barked Simon.

"I'll help Sam with the clothes,"
said Grandpa.

"I'll add the soap," said Sam.

Grandpa didn't hear Sam,
so he added some soap, too.

Then soap bubbles started to come out of the washer.
Bubbles went in the kitchen!
Bubbles went through the living room!
Bubbles went down the hall!

Simon jumped up on the chair.

"Oh, no!" said Sam. "What a mess!"

"I will make an invention to get rid of the bubbles," Grandpa said.

He stomped through the bubbles and went to the closet.

Grandpa pulled out Sara's jump rope.
He pulled out a big bag.
He pulled out an old fan and a hose.

"Hurry, Grandpa!" cried Sara.

Grandpa worked as fast as he could.

"Hold this bag," Grandpa said to Sam.

Then he asked Sara to jump rope as fast as she could.

It worked! The soap bubbles went into the bag.

Grandpa, Sara, and Sam worked
for a long time.
The soap made the house very clean!

"They're here!" called Sara
the next morning.

"Wow!" said Mom and Dad. "This
house has never looked so clean!"